7 KEYS TO BEING HAPPY WHEN TIMES ARE TOUGH

Donna,
I wish you the very best from the bottom of my heart.
love
Tosin Ayo Ajayi
Aug, 2017

By

OLUWATOSIN AYO-AJAYI

First edition published 2016

Sunshine in the Midst of the Storm™ Copyright © 2016 by Oluwatosin Ayo-Ajayi.

www.SunshineInTheMidstOfTheStorm.com

All rights reserved. No part of this publication may be reproduced, stored in a retrieval system or transmitted, in any form or by any means, electronic, mechanical, photocopying, recording or otherwise, for public or private use–except for "fair use" as brief quotations embodied in articles and | reviews–without prior written permission of the publisher.

Limit of Liability/Disclaimer of Warranty: The author of this book does not dispense medical advice or prescribe the use of any technique as a form of treatment for physical, emotional, or medical problems without the advice of a physician, either directly or indirectly. The intent of the author is only to offer information of a general nature to help you in your quest for emotional and spiritual well-being. In the event you use any of the information in this book for yourself, which is your constitutional right, the author and the publisher assume no responsibility for your actions.

Published by: Oluwatosin Ayo-Ajayi

10-10-10 Publishing, Markham, ON, Canada

Cover design by Pixelstudio

Cover image: www.depositphotos.com

ISBN: 978-0-9948597-2-3 (paperback)

ISBN: 978-0-9948597-0-9 (ebook, Kindle)

ISBN: 978-0-9948597-1-6 (ebook, ePub)

CONTENTS

DEDICATION vii
ACKNOWLEDGEMENTS ix
FOREWORD xi
PREFACE xiii
PART 1: INTRODUCTION 1
    The Storm 4
    My Background 5
    The Game of Life 7
    What is Happiness? 8
    Sources of Happiness 9
PART 2: THE KEYS 11
KEY 1: CONNECT WITH THE SPIRIT WITHIN 13
    The Response 14
    The Connection between Vibration and Happiness 14
    The Effect of Vibration on Matter: An Experiment 15
    How Does Vibration Occur? 15
    Why should you connect with the Spirit within? 16
    How do you connect with the Spirit of God within? 17
    Connecting through meditation 17
    When to meditate 18
    The meditative mode 18
    Toolkit for connecting 19
    Is praying the same thing as connecting? 20
    Some limiting beliefs about connecting through prayer: 21
    I have connected. What next? 22

Contents

KEY 2: MAKE A DECISION TO BE HAPPY **25**
    The Power of Decision Making 25
    Why is decision making important? 26
    Why is a decision for happiness important? 27
    Change your perspective about the storm 28
    Remove your focus from the storm 29

KEY 3: ASSESS YOUR BELIEF SYSTEM **31**
    The connection between your vibration and your reality 31
    Why are your beliefs important? 32
    How thoughts are formed 33
    Battle of Wills 34

KEY 4: SET GOALS **41**
    Why is goal setting important? 41
    Why is goal setting important to Happiness? 42
    How to set goals 43
    Mindset for achieving goals 44
    How to achieve set goals 47

KEY 5: DEVELOP POSITIVE RELATIONSHIPS **49**
    Relationships gone sour 50
    Relationships are a very important part of life 51
    The Power of Observation 51
    See the heart 52
    Freedom to choose my relationships 53
    Toxic relationships 53
    Healthy relationships 54
    Compartmentalization of Relationships™ 54
    Benefits of Compartmentalizing 55

KEY 6: DEVELOP POSITIVE EMOTIONS 59
Be grateful 59
Show love 62
Your words breed life: An experiment 62
Forgive 64
Why should I forgive? 65
Process of forgiving 66

KEY 7: CREATE POSITIVE EXPERIENCES FOR YOURSELF 69
Celebrate yourself 69
Be kind to yourself 70
Your silent conversations 70
How do your words, intentions, and thoughts affect your reality? 71
Treat yourself well 72
Let it glide 72
Put on a different lens 73
Laugh at yourself 74
Benefits of laughter 75
Intentionally surround yourself with things that will make you happy 75
Learn something new 76
Play good music 78
What are you waiting for? 78

PART 3: EXERCISES 81
CONCLUSION 99

DEDICATION

I dedicate this book to the memory of my loving father, Dr. Olutayo Odufalu who gave me the greatest gift of all: he taught me how to connect with the Spirit of God within.

ACKNOWLEDGEMENTS

I wish to acknowledge the following great people without whom this book would still be locked up somewhere in my mind wishing for it to become manifested.

A special thank you to Raymond Aaron who developed the program that provided the framework and support that brought this book to light. Sincere thanks also go to Andrew Brooke of the Raymond Aaron Group: my personal book architect who did not grow tired of encouraging me and always following up with me. I thank Liz Ventrella and all the staff at the Raymond Aaron Group for providing the support I needed.

I appreciate the work of Emer Gary for editing this book.

To my darling mum, Folabo Odufalu: Thank you for your prayers and words of encouragement during my down moments.

And to my sweetheart, Odeniyi Ayo-Ajayi, my greatest cheerleader who stood by me through the raging storms and motivated me to think big. I love you.

FOREWORD

It is said "experience is the best teacher." However, I say- "You don't have to experience something yourself; you can learn from other people's experiences and use it as a springboard to propel yourself into success." This is the main purpose of the book, *Sunshine in the Midst of the Storm: 7 Keys to Being Happy when Times are Tough*. Oluwatosin is excited to share her experiences; the dramatic change that came about in her life just by changing some of her beliefs, attitudes and behaviors. Health issues which she had for more than 10 years, disappeared within a period of 6 months. What happened? She is so excited to share her experiences and the changes she had to make through the pain, the sadness and frustrations to become someone full of life, energy and excitement, even in the face of challenges. She made some discoveries during the process, which she summarized as "HAPPINESS is KEY to living a HEALTHY and SUCCESSFUL life."

Oluwatosin Ayo-Ajayi is a Life Coach and Public Health specialist who has participated in several community development projects, promoting healthy behaviors among people from all walks of life. However, it is one thing to teach from a theoretical point of view and another to teach from experience. Oluwatosin has written a book in which she has combined both theoretical and practical real life experiences to demonstrate that you can actually live a happy life. The book shows you why happiness is important for living a healthy and successful life and also teaches you practical ways of how you can be happy.

In *Sunshine in the Midst of the Storm*, you get stories that bring to life scenarios which you are probably experiencing presently or

Foreword

that you can relate to; with simple practical exercises which you can implement immediately to start your journey to living a life of happiness. The book provides you with the necessary tools to face tough times when they arise, so that you are facing such times with renewed energy and get out of them faster and more triumphantly.

Sunshine in the Midst of the Storm is a message of hope; that you also can live a life full of possibilities. You can live a happy life, even if you are going through tough times. The book is full of inspiring stories, powerful insights and proven principles. It is a MUST read for anyone who is interested in living a life of peace, hope and happiness. My advice is that you read this book with a commitment to take back what rightfully belongs to you– YOUR RIGHT TO HAPPINESS!

………..*Raymond Aaron, New York Times Top Ten Best-Selling Author*

PREFACE

And the sun shone through the storm and by the time I realized it, the storm had disappeared…

8 GREAT LESSONS I LEARNED

1. My life is my responsibility and no one else's; not my parents, not my friends, not my spouse's and not God's

2. I have the freedom and power to make my life what I want it to be

3. My world is created by what I allow to enter my mind

4. A little step at a time in the right direction will take me to my destination

5. I already have the resources I need in my life. They are within me

6. Being grateful is the catalyst that will catapult me into success

7. Learning to forgive and forgiving is the magic to living a peaceful life

8. Failures and setbacks are like fire that makes gold valuable. I am very valuable and unique because I carry with me experiences that are priceless and of very great value.

7 RESOLUTIONS I MADE

1. I have decided I am going to be happy every moment of my life, in spite of any challenges that may come my way

2. I am invincible

3. I have the freedom and right to allow or disallow anyone into my space

4. I will control whatever I can control and make a declaration of what I want to God regarding what is beyond my control

5. I will not be offended by what anybody does to me. It is not worth carrying useless baggage within my soul

6. I will take baby steps everyday towards my goal and celebrate myself along the way for each successful step I take

7. I will spread a touch of kindness to whoever comes my way; one person at a time.

PART 1

INTRODUCTION

> "You are what you are and you are where you are because of what has gone into your mind.
>
> You change what you are and you change where you are by changing what goes into your mind."
>
> —*Zig Ziglar*

INTRODUCTION

It was the summer of 2015, June to be precise, in Calgary, Canada. I was seated by the window of my apartment basking in the reflection of the sun as it shone through the splitting blinds. The weather was beautiful. The sun was shining very brightly. I looked on blindly as the birds perched on the trees and hopped from one end of the yard to another, making their whistling sounds that seeped through the air like keys from a piano. I was very oblivious of my environment, gazing outside through the window, but being very far away. I was lost in thought. Unconsciously, a deep sigh escaped from me as if a heavy load had just been lifted off my shoulders.

As I returned from my journey of thought, reminiscing about the not too distant past, I noticed tears rolling down my face. Filled with an emotion of gratitude, I looked at myself and my surroundings; and as if being struck by a flash of lightening, a new awareness eroded my consciousness as if I was seeing myself for the very first time. I have changed. There was definitely something different about me. I can honestly say I am happy and content, full of life and energy, hopeful and living.

So what changed? What was it? What happened to me? Looking back in retrospect that was the day I made the decision that in spite of whatever challenges I may be facing, I am going to be happy because I deserve to be happy. So much so that I made a mantra out of it that- "In spite of all- be happy." The challenges in my life had gone on for so long that it was never ending, like a storm that had refused to stop, a dark tunnel that had been undulating- with no sign of light on the horizon.

Introduction

The Storm

The storm in my life had been going on for more than 10 years. Nothing in my life was working. I had serious health issues, was in deep financial crisis and my relationship was in a mess due to betrayal and being back-stabbed by close friends. People, both superiors at work and associates trampled upon me as and when they liked. As a result, I started hiding from life. I was just existing, like a zombie and not living. Though like a lot of us do, I moved around with a mask over my face, smiling at people and when asked, "How are you?" I replied, "Fine, thank you." But was I really fine? I knew all was not well…

I can remember just a few months ago, in November 2014, I was on the train and looking out of the window. Tears filled my eyes and I was holding them back, trying hard not to blink so that the person seated beside me would not see me crying. I was so tired of life that I did not know where or who to turn to. I took out my phone and started composing a text message. To whom, you may ask? Well, to no one else but God.

Highlight of the text message is as follows:

"……. I am tired of it all
When will all this come to an end?
I have no one to turn to. I feel all alone
I want this bleeding to stop.
I want to be comfortable
There's no one to help me
I just want to be happy
I know You are good
Please help me….."

My reaction was very funny, even to myself. I pressed on the 'send' button of my phone and the message went through. I waited a bit to see if it would bounce back. It did not. I was surprised. "Where did it go?" I wondered. "Did it actually go to God?" I asked myself. This act jolted me out of my misery. The tears dried up at once! My heart began to beat rapidly, so much so that I could hear it pounding. What did I expect? I didn't even know. I looked at my phone throughout the day to see if the message would bounce back. Well, it did not. But something did happen…

You may want to know why I composed and sent a text message to God. What was going on in my mind?

My Background

I am the second child and only girl of a family of six; including my mum and dad. I was born and raised in Nigeria, Western Africa. I lived virtually all my life in Lagos, Nigeria until I moved to Calgary, Canada with my husband in 2012. My family was one that I would describe as average middle class; a very loving and close-knit family. My father was a university lecturer and my mother worked in the same university as my father, but in administration. Growing up was full of challenges. We had so much love, but lived virtually from hand to mouth. It was during the military regime, when university lecturers were paid nothing but a pittance for pitching their tents in the great corridors of learning. We grew up without any of the luxuries of life, but with lots of love and values for living. My father was very strict and did not fail to discipline us when necessary, but I was the apple of his eye.

My parents brought us up in the Christian faith and with very high moral standards. We prayed together and read the Bible every

Introduction

morning and night before going to bed. We also had what we called the Family Forum, instituted by my father. Whenever anyone of us, either us children or our parents, had any issue with anyone of us, we brought it to the Forum and trashed the issue out there. I can remember a time when we, the children, called a Family Forum because of our father. I can't remember exactly what the issue was, but we felt he needed to apologize to us. With everyone seated, including my mother, and one of us children chairing the meeting, he gave his explanation of what happened. Every one of us gave our comments and our father's explanation made sense to us. We were only then able to see things from a different perspective and the issue was resolved. At this time, the eldest among us was less than sixteen years old. The love of God flowed in our house.

Because of my background, I had a great interest in the spiritual from a very tender age. We used to attend a spiritual church where after the worship service, a prophet, who usually sat alone during the service, wrote down messages from God and this was read out to the congregation. This aroused my interest so much that I also wanted to be able to hear God and write down whatever He says. My father observed this interest in me and at the age of eleven, he started teaching me the basics of meditation.

For me, I was just having a good time; I was very excited because I was going to see God. Praying and reading my Bible was so real that I would sit down for hours meditating on the word of God, visualizing and seeing myself speaking with God and listening so that I could hear Him speak back to me. Remember, my goal was to be able to get messages from God and write them down. I achieved my goal. I saw flashes of things, which I call visions and words dropped into my spirit. I wrote these down and showed them to my parents. As a young girl, it was so much fun that it became very normal to me. I experienced the love of God so much that I spoke to Him and He always replied. It felt so good. Even up to this day I keep a journal of revelations I have received; some which have happened within a few days, some, within months, while some are yet to be fulfilled. Looking back now, I would say this is one of the greatest gifts my father could possibly have given me- teaching me how to connect with God.

I was a very reserved girl while growing up and I believed very much in hard work and had a good attitude to life. I was content with whatever my parents could afford to give me. As long as I worked hard at something and prayed, I believed I would get what I needed. And I usually did. In school, I was an 'A' student. Outside of school, I was a role model; parents used me as an example for their kids. I was the envy of my peers. I did not understand what it meant to fail, or not to be loved, or to want something and not get it. That was all news to me. Little did I know about the game called life.

The Game of Life

Let us fast forward to when I was about thirty years old. I have lived virtually all my life as a Christian and trusted in the word of God. I was about the only one among my peers that was not yet married. Well, I waited. I began to experience scorn; people said different things and gave different advice. It was as if one thing rolled into another. I started to have health issues, what I called the "issue of blood." I had heavy periods which lasted between 2 weeks to 2 months and usually caused a lot of embarrassing moments. Even people I called friends stabbed me in the back so I was afraid to let people get close to me or know anything about me. I was living in constant fear of being harmed by the people I knew. Eventually, I got married about two years later; but the "issue of blood" did not stop. I had gone to different specialist hospitals, all to no avail. Did I still pray to God? Yes, I did. As a woman in Africa, 9 months after you got married, your stomach had better start protruding with signs of pregnancy otherwise you were an object of ridicule. For me, one year rolled into two years, two into five, six, eight, and ten years after marriage. Kids yet? No. "Issue of blood" still occurring? Yes. In 2007, my husband and I lost everything we had worked for. All our savings and investments had all gone into oblivion. Nothing seemed to be working. I was working so hard and praying so hard. Anytime we tried to rebuild our life and put some savings together, something came up to destroy it again. It was as if my life was a total wreck.

The irony of life is that for someone who believed so much in hard work and prayers, who always got whatever she wanted by working hard and praying, well, this time around, nothing seemed to work. I pondered in my mind for a long time, "When will the sun shine in my life again?" Over the years, the raging of the storm continued. It seemed as if nothing could quench it, until one day…

What is Happiness?

This is one question that has been asked throughout human history by great minds- philosophers, religious leaders, and opinion leaders alike. A myriad of definitions have surfaced, all pointing to the fact that happiness is a state of being and is very subjective. You are the only one that can really say whether you are happy or not. So what is happiness? Can you really be happy? Is it possible for you to be happy all the time? What things can affect your happiness?

Researchers have described happiness as a state of subjective well-being, which is a combination of life satisfaction and having more positive emotions than negative emotions. Happiness is also described as having three parts: pleasure, engagement, and meaning. Pleasure is the "feel good" part of happiness. Engagement refers to living a "good life" of work, family, friends, and hobbies. Meaning refers to using your strengths to contribute to a larger purpose.

Modern science defines happiness as the positive range of emotions that we feel when we are content or full of joy. For some, happiness comes from the thrill they derive from achievement.

> *"Happiness is the meaning and the purpose of life, the whole aim and end of human existence."*
>
> *—Aristotle*

For me, happiness is a state of inner peace and contentment and the excitement that comes with creating something new and living a life of meaning. What about you?

Sources of Happiness

Many of us have a mental list of what we believe will make us happy: money, material possessions, career, power, good looks, fame, and so on. We go in pursuit of these, achieve them, but find out that it wasn't what we really wanted. We feel something is still missing.

In life, we tend to overestimate the importance of wealth and underestimate the role that the choices we make play in our overall

Introduction

happiness. Have you ever been in a situation where you felt that if you had more money or more material resources, you would be happier? Such thoughts usually follow trends like, "if only I had more money, then I would be able to do…, if only my house was bigger…, I would…, if only…… if only… if only… and you are filled with so much longing and frustration. On the other hand, we forget that the choices we make in life play a very important role in our happiness. We tend to believe we have no power over our lives. The truth however is that our life, whether it is a happy one or not, is controlled to a large extent by our choices, the decisions or indecisions we make in our day-to-day life.

Studies have demonstrated that having enough income to meet basic needs and to live above the poverty level is very important to happiness. However, beyond that, more wealth does not translate into more happiness. So, how can you find happiness? What do you think?

We will answer these questions in Part 2 and discuss practical steps for living a life of fulfillment and happiness in spite of all of life's challenges.

PART 2

The Keys

The Power of Keys.

When I see a key, what comes readily to mind is either a door or a vehicle. The key is used to open a door to let something out, or to lock a door to keep something safe. For a vehicle, you place the key in the ignition to start the vehicle and go on a journey.

I hope that as you apply the Keys in Part 2 of this book, you let out whatever you need to let go from your life so that you are safe as you start a new journey of happiness, peace, and success.

KEY 1

CONNECT WITH THE SPIRIT WITHIN

What we seek without is actually within...... Great words of wisdom! Mankind is so full of activities and the hustle and bustle of everyday life, seeking solutions here and there to deal with everyday problems and challenges. A lot of people believe in connections and go to different lengths to get connected with people of influence because they believe they can get things done faster and easier if they have the right connections. That is very true! Having the right connections is very crucial to success! One of the main sources of unhappiness in the face of challenging situations is having the feeling of helplessness with no light on the horizon and a lot of questions with no answers. At times we don't know how to go about things and feel stuck. If only we can STOP and CONNECT; connect with the Spirit within!

As I mentioned earlier in my background story, while I was growing up, my father taught me how to connect with the Spirit within. Firstly, let us define what the Spirit is. Some call it God, the universe, a higher self, intuition, an inner teacher, or source energy. I refer to all of these as God and will use them interchangeably in this book.

The Response

My story started when I got to the bottom of the ladder. I was TIRED of everything that was happening in my life. My spirit was in a state of anguish and I cried out to God. I sent Him a text message with my phone in the morning on my way to work. Though the scenario was very dramatic, even to me because I was surprised the text message did not bounce back, I was stating a very strong intention to the Universe and I was expecting to get a response. I did not know the kind of response I would get or where it was going to come from, but I knew I was going to get one and I knew that when it eventually comes, it was going to be the right one. Some people say: "Trust your instincts, they are usually right." I was watching out for a sign. It eventually came that evening.

When I got back home from work, I pulled out a chair to relax while narrating the day's events to my husband including the text message I had sent to God. Then before I knew it, I dozed off; it had been such a long day! I woke up from my nap and continued to relax on the chair with the intention to get up and prepare something light for dinner. Then I heard in my spirit: "We have to raise your vibration." Wow! That's the response I was waiting for. But, what's the connection between my request and the response? I wondered. It was time to do some research.

The Connection between Vibration and Happiness

What is the connection between vibration and happiness? The answer to this question ushered in the change I am now experiencing in my life. A change from sadness, ill-health, lack of motivation, lack of energy, and merely existing to one of happiness, excitement, living life to its fullest, and turning challenges into projects.

Vibration is formed by the sum total of your thoughts, beliefs, and attitudes to life. If you want to live a happy life, then your vibration must be defined by unconditional happiness and excitement. Your vibration then attracts the resources you need to achieve your goals and the happiness you need in your life. This is how the Law of Attraction works. When you are happy and full of excitement, you are vibrating at a high frequency, but the vibration of sadness, ill-health, or lack of motivation occurs at a low frequency.

The Effect of Vibration on Matter: An Experiment

I did my research and found that several studies exist in the field of Cymatics on the visible effects of sound and vibration on matter. According to the work of Dr. Hans Jenny, the pioneer of the field of Cymatics and several other scientists, when water is exposed to different vibrational frequencies, its geometric patterns change. For instance, the geometric patterns of water changed from ordinary, plain concentric circles to very beautiful and more complex geometric patterns such as octahedrons and star tetrahedrons when it was made to vibrate at higher frequencies.

The significance of water in these studies is that the human body and the Earth consist of more than 75 percent water. Therefore, the result from these studies gives an indication of the effect of high vibrational frequencies such as happiness on humans.

How Does Vibration Occur?

The question you may ask is how does vibration occur? This occurs through your subconscious mind, which I call the "engine room of manifestation."

The five senses, which I call the gateway to our lives, transmit messages from the environment to the conscious mind, which is also the seat of our thoughts. The conscious mind then sends these messages to the subconscious mind, which in turn produces our vibrations or what we call the aura. Our vibrations are the invisible, electromagnetic waves emitted from our subconscious minds through our bodies into our environment. These go into the universe, seeking it's like which it attracts back to us as our experiences. Have you ever heard of the saying, "What you seek is seeking you"? Well, that explains it.

The subconscious mind reproduces WHATEVER is imprinted upon it as our daily experiences. This can be likened to a camera and the pictures it produces. Whatever image (thought) the lens (five senses and the conscious mind) of the camera captures is stored in the memory (subconscious mind) and is then reproduced in the color lab as a picture (experiences). This is why it is very important for us to control what we focus on and allow to be stored in our minds because these in turn form our beliefs and attitudes, and ultimately, determine our experiences.

We will discuss how our thoughts, beliefs, and attitudes affect our happiness in Key 3 of this book.

Why should you connect with the Spirit within?

- Flow of energy: If you are low in energy and demotivated, where else can you get energized if not from the Source Energy himself? Whenever I connect with Him, I experience a flow of energy and receive inner strength from within. Inner strength is what most of us need to remain calm and be able to overcome whatever challenges we are facing.

- Problem solving: I had a big problem with my life, as I mentioned earlier in this book. I had issues to deal with left, right and center. I didn't know what to do or how to go about changing it. I connected with the Spirit and a ray of light shone through the tunnel for me.

- Rejuvenation of both your spirit and body results in a feeling of wholeness. This is very important for me especially when I have a feeling of emptiness within me

- Fresh ideas: Are you devoid of ideas or need answers to some questions? Spend some time connecting with a subject matter on your mind and see whether or not you have a flow of ideas.

How do you connect with the Spirit of God within?

You connect when you are in a state of calmness in your spirit and you make Him your object of focus. This can be achieved through meditation, praying, or music.

Connecting through meditation

While there are several schools of thought on the word meditation and its benefit to us, many believe it is very mystical and metaphysical in nature. To some, the picture that comes to mind is of someone seated on the floor in a dark room with lit candles and some chanting in the background. While this may be true depending on your beliefs, for me, meditation is the act of stilling your mind from distracting thoughts and focusing on an object of interest. It is a tool which every human being must have and use. I have used this tool in major decision making to get answers on the spot and in my place of work to detect fraud. This book is also a product of meditation.

When to meditate

The best way to meditate is in a quiet place and in a relaxing atmosphere where you have the least distraction possible. While this is true when you want to make a major decision or when you are just starting out practicing meditation, the most practical time to meditate is when you need to get solutions to problems; this is usually an 'on the spot' event in our daily hustling and bustling activities. For me, I have gotten answers to very pressing issues in the oddest places- in the bathroom when taking a bath or in the toilet after doing a "major." I guess I am in the most meditative mode at these times (ah ha!). I also set aside time to meditate on a topic of interest during prayers or it may be a spur of the moment activity when I need to connect and get an answer to an immediate problem.

The meditative mode

This is a state of being connected with the Spirit within or the Source Energy until there is a flow of energy from the Source to you. It is a state of expectation; expecting to get answers after posing your questions to the Universe. For me, when I sent the text message to God in the morning, I was watching out for an answer; my listening ear was tuned in, in expectation. My answer did not come until the evening, when I got back from work. I was in a meditative mode throughout the day, even while I was working and doing my daily activities. Have you heard of the phrase: "All the answers are within?" The challenge is how to connect with the Spirit within to bring out the answers you need. You will find simple exercises of how to connect in Part 3 of this book.

Toolkit for connecting

- **Be relaxed:** You can only connect when you are relaxed. Music, whether soul-inspiring or classical music and breathing exercises can transport you into a relaxed state fast. You can also take a rest or a nap.

- **Create time to be quiet**: This can happen in a quiet environment or a place full of activities. You are quiet within yourself, with a listening ear to the Spirit within.

- **Be hopeful- don't give up but be patient**: Once you make a request, believe and expect that you will get an answer. You may not know when or how, but believe it will come.

- **Be observant:** God is always talking, the problem is we are always otherwise occupied and do not see it when the answer comes. Usually the answer comes in the most unexpected way, therefore, be observant and do not pre-empt the answer.

- **Trust the answer when it comes**: It may not be logical, it may not be what you expect but when it comes, trust that it is true. For me, answers to my request usually come in a most unexpected way. Most of the time I've had to do some research on the meaning.

For the very logical answers, I've had to put the answers to the test and observe the outcome. This has helped to build my trust over time in those types of answers.

Is praying the same thing as connecting?

Please note that I am not referring to the activities that go on in a place of worship or a religious setting as you may call it. What I am referring to is how you as an individual can connect with the Source and find solutions to your problems. I am discussing this here because a lot of people have different views about prayer.

So, what is prayer? I define prayer as a conversation and mind connection between you and a higher being. I refer to the higher being as God. Now, because we cannot see God, this type of conversation is quite different from one we engage in with someone we can see. Here, both your mind and the words being uttered from your lips must be on the same topic - you must be present. After you have spoken, you must expect a response because it will come. Can you imagine yourself in a conversation with your friend and after you spoke, you just walked away? That means you were not in a conversation, since only you spoke. A conversation is always two-sided.

While it is very good to pray, and I love to pray, the most important part of prayer is when your mind is connecting with the Spirit of God; and not the mere movement of lips. That is, both the words from your lips and your mind are focused on the same subject and you can feel a flow of energy into you. You will know when you connect because you will have a feeling of wholeness and calmness within you. However, most of the time, the lips are uttering the words while the mind is very far away from the object of prayer. For instance, compare someone who spends two hours in prayer but did not connect at all and another who spends twenty minutes in prayer and focuses with the mind for the entire twenty minutes. The person who actually prayed effectively was the one who spent the whole twenty minutes connecting.

A lot of people pray but at the same time, have very limiting beliefs about prayer. Let us discuss some limiting beliefs about prayer.

Some limiting beliefs about connecting through prayer:

1. *I do not know how to pray*: As long as you can engage in a conversation, any type of conversation, then you know how to pray. Come the way you are and speak from your heart and also expect to get a response.

2. *It is a religious rite*: While some believe praying is a socially acceptable religious rite, very few actually believe they can connect and get answers to their requests. We are a fragment of the universe. God is the Universe. We do not need a ceremony to speak with Him. Come to Him the way you are.

3. *God does not hear me*: God knows you more than you know yourself because He created you. Your spirit is actually a fragment of His Spirit. He is the Source; however, because He gave us freedom when He created us, He will not usurp on our freewill. Therefore, He always wants us to ask Him though He knows what we want before we ask.

4. *I have to go through a pastor or a religious leader to connect with God*: If you believe that we were all created by God, then

He wants each one of us to come to Him the way we are, to bring our problems to Him every moment, every day and not wait for a special time in the week to see a religious leader to help us take our problems to God.

5. *I am not good or holy enough*: God loves all His creation. You cannot be good or holy enough for Him.

6. *I have to spend a long time praying before it can get to God:* It is not about the length of time you spend praying, but ensuring that your mind is on what you are saying and not far away focused on something else. You must also believe and expect to get an answer from Him.

7. *God must do it for me*: We want Him to take over our lives and do everything for us. While I believe miracles do exist, He will not do for us what He has given us the power to do. Your life is your responsibility. Most of the time, what He does is to bring resources your way that can help you. It's up to you to acknowledge and make use of the resources.

I have connected. What next?

When you connect with the Spirit of God, expect to get an answer. Once you get the answer, it is up to you to act on it. The shortcoming most of us have is that we do not recognize it when the answer comes because it usually does not come in the way we expect.

I could have missed life's golden opportunity if I did not act on the answer I got to my request, "We have to raise your vibration." Though I did not understand the connection between my request and the response, I took a step forward and did my research. As my findings unfolded before me, I decided to give it all it would take to reach my goal. I had to embrace CHANGE in all its ramifications.

KEY 2

MAKE A DECISION TO BE HAPPY

The Power of Decision Making

It is the cry of survival, like the one from someone who is in the deep sea and drowning, fighting to stay alive and not to be washed away by the tides of life. The greatest decision I could ever make in my life is the **Decision to be happy every moment of my life**, no matter what! It ushered in NEWNESS into my life. I had to embrace CHANGE like food and water for continued existence. When I made this decision, resources came my way and my mind was open to receiving them. I suddenly 'saw' books that had been by my bedside cupboard for some time. Motivational messages which I saw everyday 'jumped' out at me as if I was hearing them for the first time. I began to have an interest in things which ordinarily would not have interested me.

Does it mean I became perfect at once and I am in top spirit every time? Well, no! I am still human. But the beautiful thing about deciding to be happy every moment is that it **helps me to REMEMBER** when challenging situations arise. When someone makes me angry or when things do not go according to plan like when I am getting worked up about an issue or when I just feel down, the decision I have made helps me to REMEMBER! Then I start to do things in a different way and snap out of the bad mood faster. Initially, it was a struggle but with time, I got better. Now, as soon as something is happening and the atmosphere around me is changing negatively, the alarm in my head starts ringing, "Remember your decision." It's like I have set myself on an auto-alert.

Why is decision making important?

Decision making is the act of making a choice between two or more courses of action. It is something we do all the time, ranging from decisions on trivial issues, like choosing which clothes to wear or what to eat, to major issues like choosing who to marry or starting a business. The process usually involves weighing the pros and cons of the different alternatives you have before making a choice. At times you make decisions intuitively since you do not have factual information regarding the issue, you only rely on your 'gut feeling.'

Decision making is probably one of the most important skills you need in life and which plagues a lot of people. At times you find out you can't just decide on something. You want to, but something is holding you back. Some people wait until they have reached the rock bottom of their lives; when they are fed up and tired before they make a decision. Some are pro-active; they see it coming and begin the process of making a decision early enough.

So why is decision making important? Decision making denotes commitment to a particular cause. It is a state of being, which the universe recognizes once made. When you make a decision to do something, you'll be amazed at the tremendous power you have at your disposal to achieve your goal. Visible and invisible resources which you never dreamt of surface. Have you ever heard of the phrase "When the student is ready, the teacher appears?" This is because the Universe works with definiteness and never with second guessing. When you make a decision, the universe brings to you whatever you need to achieve your purpose.

Why is a decision for happiness important?

Is there any other person that can tell you the importance of happiness than me? Well, I guess some other people can also tell you, but I have experienced sadness and pain, hopelessness and uselessness; so I am in a good position to give you an idea about it. Happiness is so important to existence that the only thing I can equate it to is life itself. It is a God-given gift which we were given when we were born. However, our relationships, societal expectations, life issues, accidental occurrences, and natural events bombard us with circumstances which cause a roller coaster of internal struggles within us. Living a happy life then becomes a matter of CHOICE each one of us must make.

When you are happy:

- You are healthier because your immune system is able to fight diseases more effectively and you have a better body chemistry.

- You are more successful because you are in a frame of mind to make better decisions. Happiness breeds success.

- You are energized to take up challenges and face them squarely until you overcome them.

- You are able to avoid or fight addiction more effectively. Usually addiction is caused by a depressed psychological state in a bid to find release from the cause of worry.

- People are attracted to you and your social net worth increases. Really, nobody wants to be around sad and moody people. There are enough problems in the world; a lot of people are looking for a release of happiness. Studies have shown that your social net worth is directly proportional to your wealth. If you have a high social net worth, you can use it to your advantage and create wealth from it.

- You are more hopeful. Hope gives you the energy and courage to move on with life in spite of threatening circumstances.

Change your perspective about the storm

When I made the decision to be happy, one of the first things that occurred to me was the phrase, "When life throws lemons at you, turn it into lemonade." I decided to see the challenges I had gone through in a different way. I saw them as a learning phase in my life. I thought about the lessons I had learned along the way from these experiences and felt they have given me some wisdom in certain areas which could be of use to some other people. So, instead of the feeling of the bitterness, uselessness, and hopelessness I usually felt when I thought about my experiences, I was filled with a feeling of excitement and purpose. I had a feeling of achievement and said to myself with great pride, "Wow Tosin! You sure have gone through some stuff in your life. You've got some priceless gems in your treasure box!!!"

So, what about you? I'm sure you do have some "priceless gems" also. So instead of going around gloomily counting your misfortunes, why not see them as the gems that they are and turn your lemons into lemonade?

Remove your focus from the storm

Re-focus is the word! I learned that whatever you focus on is what you are applying your energy to and that is what you will re-create a thousand-fold! I used to focus on my challenges most of the time with a lot of bitterness and regret. I talked about all the wrongs that people had done to me. I thought about the financial crisis I was going through. I thought about the ill health with a feeling of hopelessness. Though I wanted to be happy, my thoughts and actions were focused on my circumstances.

However, when I made the decision to be happy, I decided to re-focus. Now, because I had changed my perspectives, I removed my focus from my challenges and started to focus on the new things I had decided to do- to share my experiences and show people how they can avoid the mistakes I had made. At this point, I hadn't yet realized the major changes I was going to experience in my life. The mere thought of me sharing my 'lessons learned' with people charged my spirit with excitement.

> *"Tough times will pop up at one time or another. It is how we choose to respond to challenges that come our way that determines whether we are happy or not.*
>
> *What challenges are you facing presently? How are you responding to them?"*

KEY 3

ASSESS YOUR BELIEF SYSTEM

Recall that I mentioned earlier that I sent a text message to God when I felt at the very bottom of my life; when I was in distress and did not know what to do or where else to go. Well, the response I got was, "We have to raise your vibration." I did not know what this meant or what its connection to my request was. I wanted happiness and I got a response- raise your vibration. This led to my research on the connection between happiness and raised vibration.

The connection between your vibration and your reality

Your vibration is a summation of your thoughts, belief system, and attitude. It is your vibration that actually attracts the resources and circumstances that forms your current reality. High vibration is made up of positive thoughts while low vibration comprises negative thoughts. For you to be happy, your thoughts, beliefs, and attitudes must be congruent with ones that will attract happy circumstances into your life. If you are unhappy, it means you are operating at a level of low vibration.

When I had this revelation, I knew it was time for battle, but not with bows and arrows; with my BELIEFS which are already a part of me. However, I was willing and ready! The battle ground was my mind. You know at times in life when you get to the end of the road, the only other way forward is to turn back. I was already at that stage in my life. I was at the end of the road and I had made a decision, "Enough is enough! I'm done with the kind of life I am living. It's time for me to be happy!" I knew I had work to do. It was time for self-reflection. It was time to dig deep, uproot, and discard. It was time to LET GO of a lot of things. I had to identify those things that do not give me joy. I also had to determine what makes me happy. I discovered that ALL the answers were WITHIN me. It all starts with my THOUGHTS.

Why are your beliefs important?

Similar thoughts formed over a period of time become your BELIEFS and are demonstrated through your ATTITUDE. These together form your vibration. Your vibration is an electromagnetic field that surrounds you. Some call it your aura. You cannot see it, but some people can feel it. Have you ever entered a room with a few people inside it and immediately you retrace your steps because the atmosphere in the room is 'charged?' That 'charged' feeling is the sum total of the vibration of the people in the room.

An example was a customer I had who presented a product he wanted to return for cash. He did not have his receipt nor did he remember when he purchased it. I could sense that he felt I wasn't going to accept the product and I could feel anger emanating from him. I politely explained the return policy of the company and told him to give me a moment to ask the manager how we could help. When I came back and before I could open my mouth to speak, he burst out saying, "That's what people do to me everywhere I go. You're only interested in selling your product...." He went on and on. I was dumbfounded!

This man was walking around with anger and had the belief that wherever he went, people would act in a certain unfavorable way towards him. That was his subconscious expectation. Though in this case, the company was going to accept the product, his expectation had a greater hold on him and he left without fulfilling his desire - he walked away with the product.

Your reality is created through your vibration, which is a direct reflection of your beliefs and thoughts. So, change your THOUGHTS and change your LIFE.

The question is how are thoughts formed? Are you and your thoughts the same? Do you have any power over your thoughts? How can you change your thoughts?

How thoughts are formed

Thoughts are formed when our senses transmit messages from our life's events, our relationships, the environment, societal values, and expectations into our conscious minds. Thoughts which have been validated over time become beliefs and these are embedded into the subconscious mind to create our experiences. This means you and your thoughts are two different entities. YOU have the power to determine what YOU will validate to be true or not; by being intentionally aware of your thoughts as they are being formed. When a negative event occurs to me, I am aware that the default is for me to re-play the event several times in my mind. Unconsciously, I am forming beliefs about this and this is being stored in my subconscious. The solution to this is that I intercept my thoughts through auto-suggestion. I decide to give the negative event a positive interpretation and repeat it several times to myself until I believe it.

What about the limiting beliefs that were already stored in my subconscious? What should I do with them?

Battle of Wills

I knew one of the greatest battles I had to fight in life was the battle of the mind. The struggle over limiting beliefs and strong mindsets that had become part of me, so much so that I was not aware they were the cause of pain and lack of progress I was experiencing. If I can win the battle in my mind, then nothing can stop me from achieving my goal. And the battle began…

1. **Life is not fair**

I had a strong belief that life was not fair and that everything in life was controlled by destiny. This was reinforced by a Nigerian proverb that says "Fingers are not equal." This means that some people are born with fortunate circumstances; for example, they have rich parents, and things go smoothly in life for them without any hitches while it is the other way round for some other people. You can imagine the category I believed myself to be in. For instance, I was sick a lot of times, my finances were in shambles, and my relationships were nothing to write home about. I was a good player of the blame game: I blamed God, "Why did He allow all these mishaps to happen to me? After all, I served Him diligently from when I was a young girl." I blamed friends who stabbed me in the back. I blamed myself, "Why was I so unfortunate in life?" To me, I just existed on planet Earth. I operated with a victim mentality. I believed I had no control over whatever comes my way. "Things just happen," I used to think. It was meant to be.

You have the power: Break the chain!

When I got the message, "We have to raise your vibration," and with the findings from my research that my vibration is directly related to my thoughts, I realized my life is my responsibility and no one else's. Not my parent's, not my friend's, not my spouse's and not God's. Yes, I said not God's. What do you think? I realized that God will not appear and point a wand at me and say, "Vibration change! Tosin, be happy!" That will not happen; it can only happen in fantasy land! If I wanted a change in my life, I had to be prepared to change. My thoughts are manifested through my beliefs and attitude to life; these must change. God can only help me by bringing resources my way. It is entirely up to me whether I make good use of the resources or not.

You will not believe how I felt when I learned that my life was my responsibility. It was like cold water splashed over my eyes. I suddenly became alert! My eyes opened. Wow, I had power! I can control my life. I am the captain of my ship. It means when life throws unpleasant darts at me, it was my responsibility to maintain my happiness. So, my mantra changed from: "Life is not fair" to "My life is my responsibility."

2. **I have no choice**

This is one of the greatest lies of all time, "I have no choice." It is a belief that literally blindfolds you and keeps you from moving forward. I struggled with the belief that I had no alternative to the way I was living my life. I was living it the best way I could based on my circumstances. My circumstances controlled my life; financial issues, ill health, and no social life with all of these leading to sadness, pain, and depression. I did not think there was any other thing I could do. I have tried several things. I have prayed so hard, all to no avail. What else could I do? I felt I had no choice.

The power of a fresh start

Let us start from the very beginning. I decided to let go and began to pull down the stronghold of limiting beliefs that had engulfed me and were deep seated in my subconscious mind. I made up my mind for a fresh start and changed my beliefs. I dug the soil to uproot the tree and did not just cut the tree from its stem. I told myself: "I have a choice and I have the power to make the choice." Then I began to experience change in my life.

What about you? Are you experiencing sadness or pain at present? Do you feel you have no alternative to the life you are living now? A great lesson I learned is that you always have a choice. There is an alternative to what you have or what you are doing right now! There is so much power in a fresh start because you will never know if something great is awaiting you until you let go. So what are you holding on to that is giving you a lot of unhappiness? Let go of the belief that you have no choice and experience change in your life.

3. **Some people are out there to harm me; I don't want them to know anything about me.**

This was about the greatest stronghold of my life - fear of being targeted for harm. It was like being bound up and put in a cage. I had some bad relationships in the past; people I called friends back-stabbed me so much that I found it difficult to trust. As a result, I was not on any social media nor did I contribute to any discussion on the web. Not because I did not want to, but because

I lived with the notion that I was being monitored. I did not want anything about me to be mentioned in public because I did not want certain people to have access to my information. This was not about privacy; I was living in fear and did not know it. I felt I was just being careful.

This belief hindered a lot of things in my life. Something on my inside wanted to burst out for expression; I had a lot of dreams which I ALLOWED to be buried because the limiting belief was too strong.

My turnaround

The turnaround happened when I intentionally changed my belief to "I AM INVINCIBLE." I constantly affirmed to myself that I cannot control what other people do or think, but I can control what I do and think. NOTHING can happen to me unless I ALLOW it. WOW! Do you know the difference between bondage and freedom? I do! I felt so light and free. FREEDOM is good! Freedom is sweet! The feeling is like closing your eyes in a garden full of flowers with the cool breeze of fresh air blowing on the tip of your nose as you savor the scents of the flowers present in the atmosphere.

This singular change of belief has led to the manifestation of great things in my life. One of which is this book. I have a website and I am on social media with my pictures and videos on them. I am leading a movement to inspire people to live a happy life. I am reaching out to the world and living my dream. You know what, I am unstoppable!

I learned that circumstances happen to you in life; you will meet different types of people at different points in time. One of the greatest tools you can ever have is being OBSERVANT. What do people do or say to you in their unguarded moments? Is it something that shows a red flag? What do you do about it? Do you just ignore them? Like I said earlier, your life is your responsibility and no one else's. I ignored them in the past and eventually I was backstabbed. It did not come to me suddenly. We will discuss more about this in Key 5: Building Positive Relationships.

4. **I am not good enough, I have nothing to offer**

When you have been battered and nothing seems to be working for you, when you are going through tough times and it seems you have nothing to show for all your efforts, there is the tendency to walk in self-doubt and believe you are not good enough. You feel you have nothing to offer the world. Well this is a lie from the pit of hell.

Like I said in my background earlier on, I was an 'A' student in school and believed so much in hard work with prayers. Things usually worked in my favor until I began to have issues in life. Practically nothing in my life was working and people began to make mocking remarks. This went on for so long that unknowingly to me self-doubt started to creep into my subconscious. For someone who was very self-motivated and full of dreams, I got to a stage where I no longer believed in myself. Nothing I did was good enough in my own eyes. I couldn't even dream about anything. The only future I saw was living each day as it comes; I did not think I had anything to offer anybody.

I am more than I think of myself

It was December 2014. I was at the train station in Calgary, Canada coming from work and waiting for my husband. We were to connect and attend a seminar on self-development together. While waiting, I got talking with a man seated by my side. He was middle-aged, looking rough and unkempt and had a backpack by his side. From our conversation, I learned he had no place to stay, had gone through a serious health problem during which he was abandoned by people he called friends. He was constantly living in fear of loneliness so much so that he jumped into any kind of relationship which usually ended badly. He was tired of life and did not believe anybody liked him for who he was. I listened attentively, interjecting only when I wanted to empathize with him.

Then I got talking about my experiences. I connected with him through the challenges I had gone through and told him I had made a decision: "To be happy every moment of my life, no matter what!" While I was still telling my story, tears started rolling down his face. He looked at me and said: "You have so much love in you. No one has done this for me before. I cannot believe you can sit beside me and tell me all of this." Then I held his hands, smiled and said, "John, God loves you" (not his real name). I told him that I do not usually talk to strangers but that a nudge in me got me talking. I pointed out that his spirit probably was crying out for help and somehow, the Universe had arranged the meeting because as things turned out, my husband had a delay which coincidentally gave us enough time to talk. I got his phone number before I left to meet my husband.

This incident remained in my mind for quite a while. Here I was, without a thought to my experiences. It was just a 'down' period in my life. Little did I know that it transformed me into someone beautiful who was understanding, non-judgmental, and empathetic of other people's feelings. People had been very unkind to me, therefore, when people behave in a certain way, I find it very difficult to judge. I understand that we are at different phases in our lives. Most of us put on 'face masks' as we go about our daily activities. Therefore, unknown to you, someone whom you are meeting may be in their 'down' period at that point in time. The best you can do is show some kindness with your words and actions.

I sent a text message to John a few months later. He was very grateful for that day and sent me a picture showing himself at his workplace. He was into mining and for the first time in my life, I saw a picture of liquid gold. John got over his fear of loneliness and broke the relationship he was in, which he knew was not profitable for him. He said he was more hopeful as things were getting better for him. He had decided to take his time and looked forward to meeting someone very nice whom he would share his life with.

After this incident, I became convinced that I have a lot to offer, even if it is to just one person out there. What about you? Do you feel you have nothing to offer anybody? Do you feel useless and of no use to the world? If you do, then I have this question for you: Have you ever helped someone before? If you have, then you have something to offer. You are certainly more than you think of yourself; you already have what it takes. Be good to yourself and be good to others.

"Remove the stumbling block of limiting beliefs from your life and experience the pleasure of a fresh start."

KEY 4

SET GOALS

One of the most important things to successful living is your ability to set goals and achieve them. Goals are the standards against which you measure success. Success is defined as the achievement of set goals. If you do not set goals, then you do not have a yardstick against which you can measure success.

Why is goal setting important?

It is a very important part of success. Successful people make a statement of their intentions by writing down their goals; the masses leave everything to chance and take whatever comes their way. They believe they have no control over their lives and that a big invisible 'man' out there called destiny controls it.

The best way to set goals is to write them down on paper or in a journal and not just commit them to memory. "A short pencil is better than the best memory." Write down your goals on paper and break them down into baby-steps. Until you write them down, your goals, which are also your object of desire, are invisible. The process of writing down your goals puts you in a state of being during which you are engaging your brain and your mind in thinking, visualizing, and putting emotion into what you want. This is the first stage of manifestation.

Key 4: Set goals

Why is goal setting important to Happiness?

As we mentioned earlier, the purpose of setting goals is to measure success. Imagine yourself having a huge or very important task which is causing you sleepless nights. You have thought a lot about it, going through the task over and over again in your mind. It is a tough one and you don't even know where to start from. A practical example that comes readily to mind is the writing of this book. Like I mentioned in Part 1, I had a message which I wanted to share with the world, that is, how my whole world became transformed within a period of six months just because I made a decision to be happy every moment, in spite of the tough times I was going through. This was a new terrain for me. I did not know where to start from. I pondered on it in my mind for several days.

However, the magic started when I sat down with a pen and paper, and started to write down my goals. What was initially rumpled up in my brain began to get more clarity. Ideas started flowing through me so much that I wondered where they had been up to now. Then I broke the goal down into several action steps, at least to the best of my knowledge at that time. The first step I wrote was to get a mentor- someone who had already achieved what I intended to do. This was important so that I do not re-invent the wheel. I needed to get more knowledge and clarity with respect to my desire. You can only imagine how I felt looking at it on paper. Excitement burst out from inside of me. I was full of energy. I felt so happy and alive. That was achievement number one for me. I could see my message being shared all over the world. I still had a long way to go, but it was the first step and I was so full of joy about it. What about you? How do you think you will feel when you achieve something, especially if it is a huge or very important task?

How to set goals

I set goals using the MTO strategy, an acronym for Minimum, Target, Outrageous. It is a powerful process developed by Raymond Aaron, New York Times bestselling author that helps to ensure your success in achieving set goals. It eliminates a major problem encountered by many who are setting goals. This is saying that you'll do a certain thing by a specific period of time and if you don't, you feel bad. Usually if you feel bad doing a certain thing, there is a greater tendency to abandon it, and as such, it results in you not achieving your goals.

Therefore, instead of the usual traditional way of setting goals by stating that you'll achieve a certain goal by a certain period of time, you break the goal into three levels as follows:

- Minimum- this is what you can be counted on to achieve; based on your actual history of track record and not based on your hopes and desires

- Target- this is your typical stretch

- Outrageous- this is what you know you cannot achieve yet

This strategy usually guarantees success because at the very minimum, you will achieve one of your goals. This gives you a good feeling and acts as motivation for you to continue. You may want to ask, why should you set an outrageous goal if you know you cannot achieve it? Well, a lot of people have been known to go beyond their 'Target' to achieve their 'Outrageous' goal; therefore, it is not altogether unachievable.

I normally use the MTO strategy to set monthly goals, a habit I picked up at Raymond Aaron's Monthly Mentor program.

Therefore, my 'Minimum' goal for the next month is usually different from the previous month. You can use this strategy to set your short-term, mid-term, or long-term goals for your business, personal development, health, finances, spiritual development, or whatever area of life you wish.

Equally important is putting in place a support system that will aid you in achieving the goal. This is someone whom you can be accountable to.

An example:

Month 1: I have the desire to write a book on personal development

- Minimum: To gather the materials needed for the book from different sources.
- Target: To outline a framework for writing the first draft of the book. This will include chapters, topics, sub-topics, and bullet points.
- Outrageous: To write four chapters of the first draft of the book.

Support required: I will ask my husband to ensure I sit at my working desk when I get back home from work.

Mindset for achieving goals

Although goal-setting is important for success, the main purpose is to achieve set goals and before you can do this, you need to have the right mindset. Some of the important mindsets to have are discussed below:

1. **Start it:** Remember the saying, "Whatever is worth doing is worth doing well." I can vividly recall a day I was listening to Les Brown on YouTube and he said, "Whatever is worth doing is worth doing badly." "Wow," I thought, "that is new." Why should I set out to do something badly? I wondered. Then he explained, whatever your goals are, START it. Just DO IT- like the NIKE slogan. Don't over-analyze. Avoid the 'analysis to paralysis' syndrome where you analyze over and over again to the extent that you fail to take action. For me, that was huge and provided me with a great shift in mindset because that was exactly what I used to do. Now, once I've gathered enough information, I take the big leap and start the implementation of the project. However, I ensure I continue learning along the way. The lesson I learned from this was not to wait for everything to be perfect before you embark on a project; start and perfect it along the way.

2. **Set out to have fun and enjoy yourself along the way:** This is very important because you may get frustrated with some issues that may arise while trying to achieve your goal. If this occurs, it may deplete your energy level and can lead to abandonment. Therefore, inject some fun into your task. I, for instance, love to plan and expect things to go according to plan, otherwise, I get frustrated. When this happens, I remind myself that this is a journey on which I am supposed to enjoy myself. I tell myself- "Tosin, relax" and leave the task for some time. I try seeing myself the way I will be once my goal is realized. This gives me a boost of energy and excitement and I am ready to work again. The

idea is to create your fun and keep your excitement levels up while working on your goal.

3. **Be prepared to re-strategize:** Be aware that at times, things may not work out the way you planned. Remember that in life, there is no such thing as failure when you are trying to achieve a goal. The only failure is in the person who fails to try. No matter the number of times you fail at something, you are NOT a failure; you have only learned the different ways of how not to do a certain thing. That is what makes you an expert. So if you try to achieve a goal a certain way and it does not work out, try another way. NEVER give up. Keep at it because you are closer to the end than you think.

4. **It is a journey to making you a better person:** In the process of achieving a goal, starting from the point of setting the goal to its implementation, a lot of things you did not plan for may arise. You may be offended by co-workers, frustrated by issues, or discouraged by family and friends. You need to set out with the mindset of becoming a better person otherwise, these issues may give rise to negative emotions, which in turn may lower your energy and turn you into a bitter person. For me, the mere thought of who I am becoming gives me excitement and keeps me on track. Who I want to become while achieving my goal is someone who shows love and kindness to people. Different people are at different seasons in their lives; a lot of people are dealing with issues and need some help. I was there myself. Do you know that you are still in the process of 'becoming?' Well, set that goal and take action to achieve it and together let's take the journey into the land

of discovery!

5. **Be grateful:** If you want to be in a state of happiness while achieving your goals, you need to have the spirit of gratitude each step along the way. Being grateful also gives you renewed energy, the right perspective, puts you in the right frame of mind to be able to identify right strategies, and keeps you on track.

How to achieve set goals

The aim of setting goals is to achieve them and experience the thrill derived from that achievement. However, a lot of us find ourselves gone past the goal setting stage and somehow cannot continue; procrastination becomes the order of the day. Below we discuss how you can achieve set goals in spite of obstacles.

Overcome inertia: You have written the goals down, you have gathered enough information, and suddenly you develop cold feet. Something is holding you back. You think you have not prepared well enough or probably you fear change. You just want to remain where you are or keep doing what you are already used to. Well, this is a natural phenomenon. It is a demonstration of Newton's first law of motion, also called the Law of Inertia. The question is, "How do you overcome this?" To be able to overcome inertia, you need to apply a force. This can be achieved by:

Check your schedule and create space for the project: Probably your 24 hours is already full of activities and you are finding it difficult to squeeze in the new project. You have to be very practical here. Like the Law of Inertia, you either remain at a place of rest or keep doing what you are already doing and not start the new project. What I did was to make a list of my activities for a week so that I can see and visualize how my week looks and then prioritize my most important activities. Afterwards, I take the paper on which my goal, already broken down into baby steps, was written (this brings back the power of writing on paper discussed earlier) and replace some of my less important activities.

Get support: I had a goal; I wanted to share my message with the world. However, where do I start from? I had to get support. I got a mentor who provided the clarity I needed for my message to go out. I enrolled in a program my mentor was offering and the product is this new book you are reading. I also had a personal book architect, who followed up with me and encouraged me all the way. I asked questions when I got to a roadblock and got the clarity I needed to move forward.

Getting support is probably one of the smartest things you can do to achieve set goals. It was news to me when I learned that my mentor had mentors for every area of his life. Most of the big names out there also have personal coaches for different areas of their lives. So what are you waiting for?

Support can be from someone who ensures you sit at your desk and get to work on your project when you come back home from work or someone who calls you out in the morning for a jogging exercise. This is because the main challenge most people have is getting started; things get easier once you start because the momentum keeps rolling.

> *"REMEMBER, you haven't started until your goal is written on paper"*

KEY 5

DEVELOP POSITIVE RELATIONSHIPS

Your relationships will either break you or make you. This is very true to life. How do you relate to yourself and how do you relate to others? Firstly I had to deal with myself in this area. I used to give in to the whims and caprices of other people's opinions; what other people said or felt was more important that my own. I did not feel my ideas and contributions were good enough.

I looked at myself I thought, "When did I become like this? I never used to be like this." Though I was a reserved person, I used to be bold and strong. I used to believe in myself, and was full of dreams with the motivation to accomplish them. But somewhere along the way, I lost it.

I had to tell myself, "I am a human being existing on this planet. God has deemed it fit for me to exist in the universe at this point in time because I am an important person in the scheme of things. As long as I am on this planet, I am very important; and so are my ideas and contributions." I said this to myself over and over again until it became a part of me.

Key 5: Develop positive relationships

Relationships gone sour

I love to motivate people to dream and realize their dreams. I was very trusting because I felt people should love and think well of one another. I did not believe otherwise until experience taught me differently. In the past, while in Nigeria and before I got married, I had one or two friends who were very close to me, like sisters. I invited them to my home, that is, my parent's home as we were living on the university campus where my father was an associate professor. We were together for between six and eighteen years. We did things together, were very open to one another, shared our hopes, and helped one another to fulfill our dreams. For instance, when I was seeking admission for my Master's degree, one of them obtained the application form and also submitted it for me. Things went on smoothly until I started to observe unusual occurrences. I brought them up with my friends and discarded them as nothing important.

When we got married, our families became family friends; at least, that was what I thought! For example, there was an opportunity to purchase a plot of land at a discounted price through the cooperative at my place of work. I was not interested so I told my friend about it. They were able to purchase the land through me. On her own side, whenever such opportunities came up for them, she was quick to show me their purchases when the prospects were no longer available. I didn't feel good about it. I wondered: "When did this start? We used to help one another?" Well, I let it pass; we were still friends.

On different occasions, I had allowed sentiments to override my intuition. An incident occurred when those I called my friends wrote a petition against my husband and I regarding something we knew nothing about. It was very heart wrenching for us.

This affected me so much that I found it very difficult to trust; the mere mention of the word friend set me on the edge. Over the years, I asked myself: "What went wrong? At what point did things change?" Little did I know that I carried the hurt and bitterness along with me. Then I began to blame myself. I felt I should have read the signs on the wall and acted on them. Well, I have decided to let go and forgive whoever had hurt me. It is now a thing of the past. I was ready to live a new life; a life of happiness and peace without being burdened with the weight of unforgiveness. I had learned my lessons; some of which are mentioned below.

Relationships are a very important part of life

As a result of the experiences I had, I became very withdrawn and did not have any friends; I did not allow anybody to get close. I had become different and was not the usual warm, cheerful, and hospitable person I used to be. I decided it was time for a turnaround; I was going back to be who I am. I wasn't going to live the life of a recluse, but I was going to develop positive relationships along the way because it is a very important prerequisite for success. I learned that you can only go so far when you are a loner. However, your success rate increases exponentially when you are in a positive relationship because your energies interact.

The Power of Observation

One great lesson I learned which I used to ignore frequently was the power of observation. Observation is THE tool with which discoveries are made. Scientists have used it over time to make inferences when experiments are conducted. Researchers continue to use it to arrive at conclusions. The ANSWER is found from observing. One question which I used to ask myself was: "How do I know when someone I called a friend can no longer be called a friend?" I got my answer: through observation. For instance, when I started to notice some changes in the fabric of our friendship, I ignored it. When those changes became more frequent, I became sentimental and explained it away because they were my friends. When people I called friends made shocking remarks in their unguarded moments, which gave a hint of envy, I told myself to show love. I learned the hard way that showing love does not include being stupid.

See the heart

You can never see what is in people's hearts but you can see their actions which give a reflection of what is in the heart. Most especially I learned that for you to really know someone, observe what they say or do in their unguarded moments. You will see the signs; however, be wise to take heed. Some time ago, I heard Oprah Winfrey say, "If someone says this is who he is, it will be very unwise for you to say that is not who he is." That is, if someone shows you through his words or actions that he is a monster, it will be very unwise for you to say he is not. A lot of people have suffered a great deal because of this, including myself.

I decided I wanted a future full of people. I was going to meet different types of people with different personalities; however, I was going to use my very important tool of OBSERVATION to compartmentalize my positive relationships and cut off toxic relationships. I have the freedom to allow whosoever I want to be in my space.

Freedom to choose my relationships

Firstly, how you live your life is your responsibility and your relationships are a very important part of it. Due to my experiences, as a result of negative relationships, I found it very difficult to trust or allow people get close to me. This caused a lot of stress and unhappiness for me because I know that developing good relationships is very important to my success, but I was living in fear. I felt I wouldn't know how to cut off an unhealthy relationship with a friend if I found myself in one, so instead, I decided it was better for me not to have one at all. I used to allow sentiments to override my judgment and felt compelled to remain friends with people in the name of showing love to all.

When I decided it was time for me to be happy, one of the things I learned was that I have the FREEDOM to CHOOSE who I want to allow into my space. If a relationship with a friend is becoming unhealthy or toxic, I am at liberty to cut it off without any regrets. This is not about conflict in a relationship. There is a place for that - conflict resolution is an important part of bonding in relationships. I have identified some characteristics of a toxic relationship below.

Toxic relationships

The quality of your relationship is very important to your health and success. A toxic relationship is very unhealthy; it can cause a toxic internal environment which can lead to stress, depression, anxiety, and medical problems.

Characteristics of toxic relationships include demeaning comments and attitudes, jealousy, self-centeredness, criticism, selfishness, dishonesty, distrust, insecurity, abuse of power and control, and being demanding.

The best solution to a toxic relationship is to press the delete button. If it is a relationship you cannot avoid, for example a family member or co-worker, be as distant as possible. The least interaction you have with the person the better for you.

Healthy relationships

A healthy relationship is one that brings more happiness than stress into your life.

It is characterized by mutual respect for each other's opinions and values, good communication, trust and honesty, support for one another, fairness, respect for each person's sexual boundaries, conflict resolution in a rational, peaceful, and mutually agreed way, and the ability to engage in a way that eliminates manipulative, controlling, emotional, and/or physical abuse.

Compartmentalization of Relationships™

Have you heard the phrase, "Show me your friends and I'll tell you who you are?" If you mingle with happy and successful people, it will rub off on you and the same applies vice versa. Compartmentalization of relationships is a concept based on the fact that our energies interact; people who we mingle with and interact with affect the outcome of our lives. Therefore, you want to place people who have characteristics and whose relationship will be most beneficial to you in the compartment closest to you, and people with characteristics and whose relationship are least beneficial to you further away from you. Only those with whom you have healthy relationships are placed in any of the compartments; a toxic relationship is not a part of these compartments.

Benefits of Compartmentalizing

The benefit of compartmentalizing is that it helps you put into perspective the types of relationships you have at any point in time so that you can readily redefine who should be closest to you and who you should interact less with. This was what I did with my relationships. I redefined them and deleted the toxic relationships in my life.

The diagram below demonstrates relationships that should be closest to you in Compartment 1 and those that should be farthest away from you in Compartment 3

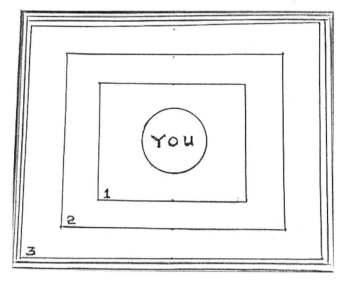

Key 5: Develop positive relationships

Characteristics of people in each compartment and their benefits to you are discussed below:

Compartment 1: People who should be in this compartment include those who-

- Have a positive attitude to life

- Share the same vision as you

- Are already successful in what you want to do

- Are encouragers and motivators

- Provide you with constructive criticisms

- Provide support for your endeavors

These people include friends, mentors, coaches, acquaintances, co-workers, or family members. You should spend most of your time interacting with them either by physical contact, on the phone, social media, or reading materials provided by them. They provide a positive influence on you and help you achieve your goals faster.

For instance, if you want to be happy and successful, these are the group of people you should surround yourself with. Be as close to them as possible, join their mastermind groups, or follow them on social media.

If you are interested in living a happy life, join the community of happy people at www.SunshineInTheMidstOfTheStorm.com/HappyLight

Compartment 2: People who should be in this compartment include those who-

- Have a positive attitude to life
- Do not share the same vision as you, but have their own vision
- Are successful in what they are doing

They include friends, co-workers, or family members who are successful in their own right. You can spend some time interacting with them because you can learn from them and the relationship can be beneficial to you in achieving your goals.

Compartment 3: People who should be in this compartment include those who have any of the following-

- You do not know a lot about them
- Do not have a positive attitude to life
- Do not share the same vision as you/do not have any vision at all
- Are discouragers or de-motivators

This group includes friends, co-workers, family members, or acquaintances. You should have the least interaction with them because they provide a negative influence on you and may detract you from achieving your goals. They may just be a number in your network.

So friends, what kind of relationships are you in presently? Who are your friends? Who do you interact most with? How beneficial are your relationships to achieving your goals? Do you have people who you spend a lot of time with, but who you should move to compartment 3 and vice versa?

Key 5: Develop positive relationships

See some exercises in Part 3 of this book which can help you compartmentalize and re-define your relationships.

> *"You have the freedom to choose who to interact with. Choose wisely."*

KEY 6

DEVELOP POSITIVE EMOTIONS

Your emotions can be described as an instinctive response to your circumstances and a demonstration of your feelings. It is very crucial to your state of well-being. Emotions can be either positive such as joy, love, and gratitude or negative such as sadness, anger, hurt, and bitterness. When you have a negative emotion, it is an indication that something is wrong somewhere. You need to find the cause of this and address it. Examine the thoughts going through your mind before and while you are going through the emotion. It gives an indication of the cause of the emotion, which you have to address in order to be happy again.

This was what I did. I had to address my situation and examined the thoughts that passed through my mind each time I experienced a negative emotion. With this, I was able to identify what caused the negative emotion in the first place. Then I intentionally developed positive emotions that helped my feelings. I have discussed some of them below.

Be grateful

Gratitude is one of the greatest emotions that can take you out of a challenging situation faster than you think because being grateful changes your perspective on things. Life and living is mainly about YOUR PERSPECTIVES. When you are grateful, you operate from a place of abundance and humility.

When I was in the state of despair and I decided it was time for me to be happy, one of the first things I learned was to be grateful especially for things I took for granted. I started to reflect and wrote a **'Taken for Granted' list.** I discovered it was a very long list. Wow! I thought to myself; I didn't know I had so much; and all the while I was filled with the feeling of lack and emptiness. It is so easy to be grateful for big things- especially when you receive a gift or get a promotion, while the small things look insignificant. But our lives are made up of small, seemingly insignificant events or people. At times, we take the significant people in our lives for granted because they are not what we think they should be.

After I wrote my 'Taken for Granted' list, the way I prayed and said "Thank you, Lord" became different. For me, thank you became THANK YOU. I saw things differently and felt so good. There was so much to be thankful for. I was thankful that I still had life. I became thankful for my experiences when it suddenly occurred to me that they could serve as a springboard for others. Someone else could learn something from the pain I had gone through. I am thankful that I am writing this book- it has created a host of great experiences in my life: I have met new wonderful people, created new relationships, learned new things, joined new groups, and I have new inspiring things to talk about. It is a very thrilling experience to see people who are discouraged glow with a light of encouragement in their eyes after talking to them. The list is endless and for all these, I am grateful.

Can you believe that there was a time in my life when I couldn't use my imagination? Though I knew about the power of imagination, I couldn't just sit down to imagine anything. When

I tried doing this, all I could see and feel was pain, pain, pain; nothing else but pain. If you are in the same shoes as I was, then give this a try.

For a start, write a 'Taken for Granted' list. This can include:

- Nature (sunshine, air, sea, ocean, vegetation, flowers)

- People at work or in your family (imagine how your life would be if you did not have them in your life)

- Your experiences: What are you going through presently, any tough times? You may think why this should be on your list? Well, there is always something to learn from any negative experience you have gone through or are going through. Your mess can become your message; just like I am doing right now by writing this book.

- Your strengths: Do you love singing, writing, talking, listening, are you a patient person, do you understand things easily? There are some people out there who do not have these strengths.

- Your weakness: What are your weaknesses? Identify them as they are a reminder that you are human and you need other people in your life.

2. Look through these and imagine how your life would have been without them

3. Say 'THANK YOU' for each of the items on your list

Show love

Love is an emotion we were born with; however, the environment has conditioned us to be very critical of ourselves and others. We need to return to being who we really are. Be kind to people and be kind to yourself because being kind is love in action. Can you say you love someone and you are unkind to them? Also, show yourself some respect and dignity. If you don't, who will? The way you treat yourself is how others will treat you.

Have you done something for which you feel you deserve to be punished? Probably you are going through a tough time or you think the tough time you are going through is a consequence of your actions. Well, it's time to let go. Show yourself some love and be kind.

If you are going to utter a word to someone, ensure it is seasoned with kindness otherwise, keep quiet.

Your words breed life: An experiment

An experiment conducted by Dr. Masaru Emoto, the renowned Japanese alternative medicine practitioner, shows the effect of the spoken word on rice. He placed rice in three glass beakers and covered them with water. Every day for one month he did the following to the beakers:

Beaker 1: He said "Thank you"

Beaker 2: He said, "You are an idiot"

Beaker 3: He completely ignored.

After one month, he made an amazing observation on the rice in the three beakers.

Beaker 1: The rice had begun to ferment giving off a strong pleasant aroma

Beaker 2: The rice had turned black

Beaker 3: The rice had begun to rot

The significance of this experiment is that the words that we speak to others or ourselves that convey positive emotions such as love and kindness breeds life, while negativity and indifference does nobody any good.

What is your personality like? I am a perfectionist. I set very high standards for myself. As a result, it takes a lot for me to see anything good in what I do. I usually feel it is not good enough. When I go below my expectations, I become very harsh with myself and blame myself for as long as I can. As a result, I put myself under a lot of stress. Well, I have made that a thing of the past! Now, I tell myself, "Tosin, be kind to yourself." "It is okay- you have tried your best." "It is okay to have weaknesses- it shows you are human and not God." When people use hurtful words with me, I do not accept it as I used to do. I remind myself that, "I do not have a problem." "Hurting people hurt people; they probably have issues they are dealing with in their lives."

Therefore friends, show love and be kind. Firstly, give yourself a Touch of Kindness and together, let us spread the Torch of Kindness to others. Be happy and together, let us spread happiness. Visit www.SunshineInTheMidstOfTheStorm.com/HappyLight to join the Happiness movement.

Forgive

When you are going through a painful period created by a relationship gone sour, an act of betrayal from friends, or an abusive boss at work whom you probably have to face every day, it is so difficult to forgive because your senses are blinded by pain. All you can think of is the hurt and pain. So how can you forgive? Is it practical to forgive?

When you feel you have sabotaged yourself or you have done something you think you shouldn't have and this has resulted in something unpleasant for you, something you probably have to live with for a very long time, what do you think? Is it okay to forgive yourself? Isn't it mild enough for you to flog yourself over and over again, at least to feel consoled that you are receiving some punishment for what you have done?

When you feel you have been faithful to God, by serving Him fervently all through your life, and somehow it seems He has turned His back on you; otherwise, why should you be going through so much pain, ill health, lack of success in your endeavors? You pray endlessly, all to no avail. No help seems to be coming from Him. Then your sensitivity to Him begins to wax cold and you conclude, "There is nothing He can do about my situation," and you slip into a state of helplessness. To you He no longer exists. Is it possible to forgive God?

Have you been in any of these three states; feeling hurt towards others, yourself, or God? Do you play the blame game; blaming any or all of the three for your misfortunes? Well, I have been there. The three scenarios above described me at one point in my life or the other. So, why should I forgive?

I am in the best position to testify to the power of forgiveness. It is so tremendous; its benefits can only be likened to the grains of sands by the seashore. Firstly, what price tag can you give to 'peace?' Is there any? I do not think so. I learned that learning to forgive and forgiving is the magic to living a peaceful life and I made a resolution that I would not allow anybody to offend me because it is not worth carrying useless baggage within my soul.

Why should I forgive?

Walking in bitterness and unforgiveness can be likened to carrying the weight of useless baggage. Is there any way you can be free of the weight unless you put it down? The answer is to LET GO and MOVE ON.

When you do not forgive, it's like capturing a painful experience in your conscious mind and intentionally deciding to relive it over and over again. Why should I do that? It's time to LET GO and MOVE ON.

Bitterness will cause physical, mental, emotional, and spiritual consequences in you. Physical consequences include hormonal imbalance from various glands thereby causing many symptoms and diseases, and a weakened immune system resulting in an inability of the body to fight diseases. Mental and emotional consequences include depression, emotional stress, fatigue, and sleeplessness.

Unknown to me, I had been living in bitterness for a long time. I felt justified because I was betrayed and back-stabbed by people I called friends. Then I blamed myself because I felt I should have seen it coming; instead, I ignored the nudging feelings I had. No

Key 6: Develop positive emotions

wonder I was going through a myriad of negative occurrences in my life! I thought to myself, at what cost would I continue to live my moments pondering on what people had done to me? The truth is, I am still going to meet a lot of people in the future and offense will come in different colors. Would I continue to be offended by what people do to me or would I want to live as a recluse all my life? I decided I'd had enough: I wanted to experience happiness and not bitterness. I love people and wanted to meet a lot of people in the future. I would have to deal with myself and find ways of dealing with offensive situations as they arise. You know why? Because I had decided I was ready to live a life full of fun. It was time to let go of the past.

Process of forgiving

How do you know if you have forgiven someone? It is when you remember the bad experience and you no longer feel the pain or hurt; you can actually laugh over it.

For me, firstly I had to engage my thoughts and feelings. I accepted the fact that a negative event occurred in my life which hurt me and caused me pain.

Then I asked myself the following questions:

1. "What have I gained by filling my thoughts with bad experiences?" I have gained nothing but ill health and depression. I had also created a stumbling block for myself. It was time for a change!

2. "Are the people who caused the hurt experiencing the same thing I am experiencing at present?" The answer to

this question caused a great shift for me and hastened the forgiving process when it dawned on me that the people who hurt me have gone on their way and continued with their lives. They are probably at the cinema or enjoying themselves in one way or the other; or perhaps they had derived some form of satisfaction from what they did. Meanwhile, I had put a halt on my life moping over the pain continuously over time. When this realization hit me, it was as if a balloon was punctured and bam! The air inside it diffused within seconds.

3. "Who will benefit from being forgiven? The people who caused the hurt or me?" I realized that the main beneficiary from forgiving is not the person who caused the pain; it is for me to be free and able to move on with my life.

People who hurt others usually have issues they have to deal with in their lives. They probably are not aware they have caused you pain because they are blinded by their problems. After checking myself and I'm sure I have not caused the reaction, I tell myself: "Tosin, you do not have problems; ……. (mentioning the other party's name) probably has problems that HE/SHE needs to sort out."

Lastly, I had to talk to myself and fill my thoughts with positive events.

"I forgive you (mentioning the name of the person who had hurt me) because I deserve to be happy. I forgive you because it is time for me to be free from any burden. I forgive you because it is time to let go of this situation. I forgive you because it is time to move on with my life. I forgive you because a lot of happy experiences are waiting for me."

"Your emotions are like magnet that attract to you a thousand-fold of your feelings and create your reality. Check your emotions regularly and choose positive emotions over negative ones."

KEY 7

CREATE POSITIVE EXPERIENCES FOR YOURSELF

You may be going through some challenges and all you want is to see an end to it. Your focus is so much on when will this come to an end. How will this come to an end? Well, as we discussed in Key 2, it is time to re-focus; remove your focus from whatever challenge you are going through. Remember, your life is your responsibility and no one else's. Just like myself, I had gotten to the rock bottom of my life; there was nowhere else to go except under. I was tired, too tired of it all.

Then I made a decision, I AM GOING TO BE HAPPY EVERY MOMENT OF MY LIFE. Did I still have the challenges then? Yes I did. Do I still have challenges now? Yes, I do. What changed? It was my disposition and perspective on life. I created positive experiences for myself. So dear friend, it is time to think about something positive for you. If you think there is nothing positive going on in your life, then create something. Use your energy for something positive for you. We will discuss some of the things you can do below.

Celebrate yourself

If you don't celebrate yourself, who will? Rest assured, nobody will. You may be asking, what is there to celebrate? I did the same.

Looking back in retrospect, with all the things going on in my life, there was nothing to celebrate. However, when I had a change in perspective, I saw myself in a different light. For someone to have gone through what I went through, I give myself a clap. What about you? If you are going through some stuff presently and you are still breathing, you sure deserve a clap! Give yourself a clap!

Be kind to yourself

- **Say positive words to yourself.**

There is nothing as true as the Power of Words; the ones you say to others, the ones you say to yourself, and the ones other people say to you. When people say hurtful words to you, it's like arrows inflicting wounds in your heart and when people say pleasant things to you, you are filled with feelings that warm up your heart. This is because words carry the substance with which we shape our lives.

- **Your silent conversations**

This is one of the least things we do; being kind to ourselves. It never crossed my mind for one moment to be kind to myself. What about you? There are a myriad of scenarios I can think of. For instance, what do you say to yourself when nobody is watching, when nobody is with you; I call it our silent conversations. You are working on an assignment and suddenly you missed it- do you say to yourself "There you go again; why can't you ever get it right?" Or what names do you call yourself when you get something wrong? "Stupid?" "Good for nothing?" You are working on a project at work and you are telling yourself: "You are too slow" or "You are ...."

Take a mental step back and watch your silent conversations; this gives you a reflection of what your beliefs about yourself are. These beliefs are deep seated in your subconscious and resurface spontaneously when triggered by events you are experiencing.

The issue is that you don't see anything good in yourself or in what you are doing. You are just too harsh on yourself! When such torrents of negative suggestions come to your mind, tell yourself "Give me a break!" and change whatever negativity you hear with positive statements.

How do your words, intentions, and thoughts affect your reality?

Dr. Masaru Emoto, the Japanese doctor of Alternative Medicine, demonstrated the effects of our speech, intentions, thoughts, and vibrations on our reality. He performed an experiment where he exposed samples of distilled water to words that conveyed either a positive or negative meaning, froze them for some hours, and then viewed them using a dark field microscope.

The experiment showed the effect of words on the molecular structure of water. Positive words such as "I love you," "thank you," "peace" showed very beautiful patterned crystals while negative words like "I hate you," "fool," "war" gave irregularly shaped and very ugly crystals.

The rationale behind using water was that both the Earth and the human body comprise over 75 percent of water. The significance of this experiment is that it shows how our bodies and our realities respond to words. Practically, if someone tells you, "I

Key 7: Create positive experiences for yourself

love you," you feel good; on the other hand, if you are told "I hate you," you feel bad.

(Bonus: Go to: www.SunshineInTheMidstOfTheStorm.com and download a free copy of the ebook: The Power of Words)

- **Treat yourself well**

How do you treat yourself? I told myself, "It is time for me to treat ME well!" People will most likely treat you the same way you treat yourself; it is usually an unwritten code. If you are working on something and you make a mistake, allow yourself to be. You are human. Learn from your mistake and move on. It is just another way of not doing things. That is how experts are made.

Learn to be confident at whatever you are doing. If you do not know how to do something, get someone to teach you. Learn, learn, and learn. You will be surprised that very successful people have personal trainers for most of the things they do. I have a coach for this book I am writing. At the very least, get materials to learn from.

You are an embodiment of greatness, waiting to be unleashed. You are more than what you think! So, treat yourself well!

Let it glide

I was watching a 'how to' video on YouTube, and an advert showing a soccer player interrupted the scene. The player did many maneuvers with the ball; he threw it up and used his head to catch the ball. He also bounced the ball on his shoulder and allowed it to glide down his back. Looking at this, I thought to myself, "How true this situation is to life, to our relationships." This is especially true when someone is throwing hurtful words at you like darts being thrown at a dartboard.

I call it "The Gliding Ball approach to dealing with Harsh Words." When someone is condescending and using very hurtful words directed at you, let the words glide over you like a ball glides over the shoulder of a footballer. Would you still see the ball staying at your back? Certainly not! Do this mentally too and actually see the hateful words slide down, then laugh over the harsh words that were lashed at you.

Put on a different lens

I was dealing with an angry customer who wanted me to bend a regulatory issue. While trying to calm him down and explain the different options available, he became very abusive. My colleagues all came round me to offer their support. Most of them could not believe how I took it and concluded I must be very strong. For me, I allowed the words to glide over me and put on my learning lens: I switched immediately to my learning mode. What I CHOSE TO SEE was how people behave when they wanted to get their way. I was observing the different transitions that occurred from the man's reactions; that is, from listening to me to flaring up.

I came out of the situation smiling because I was seeing something different. I almost did not hear the uncouth words he was using; that wasn't my focus. Instead, I was observing something about human behavior which I was going to process later. The advantage of putting on a different lens is that the sting is absent when the scenario re-plays itself in my quiet moments. Most of the time, it is the re-play of events in our minds that causes the

Key 7: Create positive experiences for yourself

ripple effect in other areas of our lives.

For me, learning something new creates excitement and passion in me; your experience may be different. The idea is for you to replace the ugly situation with something pleasant. Remember, it's all about your perspective. When certain situations arise in our lives, we react to them based on who we are and not really on the circumstances themselves. Two people facing the same circumstances most likely will have different experiences. Choose your lenses; be very intentional about this and put them on when the situation calls for it.

Laugh at yourself

Have you ever tried laughing out loud at yourself? When was the last time you committed a blunder and instead of flogging yourself, you laughed? This is one of the things I started doing consistently because I am usually very hard on myself. I do not give myself space - I believe I am supposed to be perfect. However, I asked myself, "What have I gained from this?" Nothing but stress, depression, demotivation, and a waste of time. Remember, it is all about one's perspective.

Therefore, what I do to douse the situation so that I can have my peace and move on is to laugh: belly wrenching laughter. What's your personality like? Are you someone like me? A perfectionist? Someone who has a need to be right all the time? Have you set up a high standard for yourself? When you fall short of your expectations, try this: Tell yourself, "It's time to laugh" and laugh out loud.

Benefits of laughter

Why should you laugh? Studies have shown that laughter has a lot of physiological and psychological benefits such as reducing the level of stress with its harmful effects, boosting your immune function, normalizing blood pressure, and helps to fight heart diseases. It also works to activate endorphins, which is the mood and pain relieving hormone. In fact, laughter has been described as a Universal Medicine.

According to Mariusz Wirga, Medical Director of the Psychosocial Oncology Memorial Care Todd Cancer Institute, Long Beach Memorial, choosing to set aside time each day for unconditional laughter, where jokes or humor are not needed, is the most important part of universal medicine. It helps to promote healing. Studies also show that there is a direct correlation between the amount of laughter you engage in and your overall level of health.

The best part is that laughter is free; you cannot have an overdose of it and it has no adverse side effects. So why not give yourself a dose of humor. Laugh at yourself and also help to spread laughter.

Please visit www.SunshineInTheMidstOfTheStorm.com/HappyLight to join the Happiness movement.

Intentionally surround yourself with things that will make you happy

Take a look at your immediate environment. I refer to the physical things around you and the people you surround yourself with (we have discussed the latter group in details in Key 5: Develop Positive

Key 7: Create positive experiences for yourself

Relationships). What can you see there? Surround yourself with things that will send out positive vibrations into your environment and therefore create a happy aura around you. I had a friend who had a lot of stuff going on in her life. She complained about her husband, her business, and her relationships. One day she invited me to her house and the first thing that greeted me as I entered her living room was the portrait of a lady in tears. Looking round, I could point at two other pictures that sent out sad messages. I drew her attention to this and advised that she replace them with pictures that can create joyful and positive images in her mind. A lot of us are going through one tough time or the other; why make it worse by surrounding yourself with pictures or words that create a sad environment?

For instance, what images or messages are on the walls of your house, the screen savers of your phone, or the wall paper of your computer devices such as tablet, laptop and desktop? It is very important that you are intentional about installing or putting in place messages on devices which you look at on a continuous basis.

Bonus:

Please visit www.SunshineInTheMidstOfTheStorm.com for a free download of wall papers with inspiring messages.

Learn something new

If you are going through a challenging period, it is time to re-focus. Remove your focus from the issues bugging you. Remember that you create whatever you focus upon, especially when you do it with your emotions. So learn something new. Take up a new project that will make you focus on improving yourself. There is a type of excitement that comes with the thought of doing something for yourself. However, remember that the intention is to make yourself happy at every single moment along the way. If you are getting frustrated along the way, tell yourself (mentioning your name) "......... give yourself a break." This was exactly what I did.

During the dark period of my life, I felt useless and unworthy. It was as if I was just occupying space on planet Earth. But when I learned that I was operating at a very low vibration and needed to increase this and discovered the connection between happiness and high vibration, I made up my mind that enough was enough! I began to re-focus. Life threw lemons at me and I decided to turn them into lemonade. I took up the project of writing this book and creating the Happiness movement to teach people from my experiences on how to deal with tough times and live a happy life. I can only leave you to imagine how I felt. The mere thought of contributing to other people's life gave me a surge of energy; it was an exhilarating feeling. I became alive and living; not just existing. Did I get moments of frustration along the way? Yes I did. A lot of them; I wouldn't be human if I didn't, because it was a new terrain for me. However, I had a new perspective to living. When you are starting something new, things do not usually go smoothly, not as you would want it to, because you are just learning the 'how's' and 'how not to' of doing things. But now I tell myself that that's where the excitement comes from! It is part of the story! That is who I have become when I made the decision to be happy at every moment of my life. I see challenges in a new perspective; I turn things around for myself and decide on the interpretation I want it to have. I am very intentional about the message I want to be stored in my subconscious because this will recreate my experiences.

Key 7: Create positive experiences for yourself

Play good music

Good music is medicine for the soul. Listen to some music. It has a way of calming you. Take a step further and dance. The common thing is to dance when you are happy. Have you ever tried dancing to some music when you are not happy? Try it. Tune in to some good music, put on your dancing shoes, and do the swagger! I did this and discovered a lift in my mood; I was also full of energy by the time I finished the exercise. So, why not give it a try?

What are you waiting for?

So friends, what are you waiting for? If you have a project you are working on presently, and you are experiencing some challenges or you are getting frustrated, tell yourself you are learning something new from the experience. Identify the new thing you are about to learn and be grateful for the opportunity. Do this several times until your outlook to the situation changes and you actually believe you are learning something new. This creates a new aura around you, increases your energy, and turns you from being passive to being passionate about the venture.

If you haven't started anything yet and you are tied to the challenges you are facing presently, I ask that you give yourself a try. Take up a new project and re-focus your energy. Your challenge may be job related, a health issue, a financial crisis, or may involve your relationships. Whatever it is, make up your mind to re-focus and choose to be happy in spite of your challenges. The secret is that you bounce out of the situation at a faster rate, with much more energy and become who you never thought you could be. I have been there and I testify that I experienced a turnaround in my life. What do you think? Isn't it worth experimenting?

Visit www.SunshineInTheMidstOfTheStorm.com/HappyLight to join the Happiness movement and get the support you need to live a happy life.

"If you do not make yourself happy, who will?

Do not wait for someone else to make you happy; they are probably dealing with something in their own lives at the moment.

Create your own happiness...."

PART 3

EXERCISES

Exercise 1

TAKE A STAND FOR HAPPINESS: DECIDE TO BE HAPPY!

Are you going through a tough time and are you fighting it with so much stress?

Is there a storm going on in your life and you feel you are going under?

Do you look around you and see yourself in the midst of people but you feel alone and lonely?

Well, you have more power than you think. You may not know how, you may not know when, but one thing you need is A COMMITMENT to your own happiness!

Make a DECISION today! Tell yourself; repeat this several times- "IT IS MY TURN TO BE HAPPY. I TAKE A STAND FOR HAPPINESS! IT IS MY TURN TO BE HAPPY."

Exercise 2

CHANGE YOUR THOUGHTS AND CHANGE YOUR REALITY: RE-FOCUS.

Your beliefs control your reality. Your belief system is formed from your thoughts. Change your thoughts and change your reality. The following exercises are aimed at helping you RE-FOCUS your thoughts.

The importance of this is that while you are going through or after a negative experience, the default is for you to have a random torrent of negative thoughts going through your mind. If this is not intercepted, it becomes embedded in your subconscious and starts to create an avalanche of negative events in your life such as stress, illnesses, depression, which you usually do not attribute to the negative thoughts in the first place.

However, you are in control and can operate from a position of power when you:

- Know that you are a different entity from your thoughts

- Become aware of negative thoughts immediately as they are being formed

Exercise 2

- Know that you have the ability to change your thoughts
- Can control the direction of your thoughts

Uses of the Re-Focus exercise:

- In relationships where people use unkind words with you
- When you are angry or hurting
- When you are filled with fear and you need to calm yourself

A. **Be conscious of your thoughts**

The goal of this exercise is to demonstrate that you and your thoughts are two separate entities

1. **Relax**

    a. Firstly, you want to relax by taking on a comfortable position which could be sitting on a chair, a couch, on the floor, or on the bed with pillows placed behind you

    b. Secondly, you want to relax through rhythmic breathing

Inhale slowly but deeply counting 1, 2, 3; 1, 2, 3; 1, 2, 3

Hold your breath (count 1, 2, 3)

Exhale slowly but fully, also counting 1, 2, 3; 1, 2, 3; 1, 2, 3

Repeat this exercise until you have maintained a steady rhythm and you are fully relaxed

2. **Observe your thoughts**

    a. Close your eyes while still maintaining your relaxed position and rhythmic breathing

    b. Observe the thoughts going through your mind. Do this for 5 minutes

    c. Do not try to control or change them; only observe

    d. Take note of them

You will observe that you and your thoughts are two separate entities.

   a. Your thoughts are coming to you from different sources.

   b. You are an observer

B. **Identify and take note of your thought pattern**

The goal of this step is to see your thought pattern.

   a. Make a list of the thoughts that passed through your mind in step 2 above without altering them.

   b. Categorize similar ones into groups. Is there a pattern?

   c. Where did the thoughts originate from?

   d. How many sources did you identify?

C. RE-FOCUS: Replace negative thoughts with positive ones

The main goal here is to intercept negative thoughts as they are being formed and replace them with positive ones.

   a. Once you identify a negative thought, do not push it away or tell yourself it does not exist. It exists because it has a source; otherwise, your brain may process it as a lie and this may not be acceptable to you.

   b. Instead, turn it around into something positive which is acceptable to you

   c. Repeat the positive event to yourself until you believe it and it replaces the negative thought

An example:

You are in the process of developing a message and suddenly, you develop cold feet.

Your thoughts: "I am not an expert." "Nobody will like the message."

Source of your thoughts: Other experts in the field, which are making you feel intimidated.

RE-FOCUSING statement: "Yes, there are other experts in the field, but they started from somewhere just like I am doing now. Most likely, they also developed cold feet when they were just starting out."(Laugh at yourself).

"My message may not be for everybody, but those who it is meant for will be attracted to it and it will be very beneficial to them."

Exercise 3

CONNECT WITH THE SPIRIT WITHIN

Have you heard of the phrase, "All that you seek without is within?" The goal of this exercise is to connect with the Spirit of God within you. You know you have connected with someone when you can 'feel' that person. This exercise is useful for:

- Getting close to God
- Solving problems
- Getting answers to questions
- Getting fresh ideas

The main ingredients you need are some TIME and the DESIRE to connect.

Simple Connecting exercises

1. **Relax**

Refer to exercise 'A' above: 'Be conscious of your thoughts' for the relaxation exercises.

Exercise 3

2. **'Still' your mind using the following Focusing/concentration exercise:**

a. Prepare your Focus material

   (You need a piece of plain paper, pencil, black marker, cellotape)

Get a piece of white PLAIN paper

Use a pencil and draw a large square on it. The dimensions are not important as long as it is a square. (A square has four equal sides.)

In the middle of the square, use a black marker (or any other dark colour) to make a large spherical spot.

Place the paper on the wall or on a board using the cellotape. Ensure the paper is placed at your eye level while you are seated in a comfortable relaxed position.

b. Focus on the dark spot

Focus on the dark spot counting very slowly from 1 to 10

Block your mind by ensuring no other thoughts come through your mind while counting from 1 to 10

If a thought crosses your mind, start the count all over again. (Initially, you will have thoughts crossing your mind several times. Do not be bothered about this. It is normal. Keep at it.)

Take note of your successful attempts. (A full count of 1 to 10 is one successful attempt).

10 successful attempts are OK for a day.

Do this consistently for ten consecutive days or until you are comfortable with holding your thoughts.

3. **Focus on one thought**

Repeat the relaxation exercises above.

Identify an object to focus on. It can be anything- a cup, bottle, flower... anything.

Look at the object for some time until it forms in your mind's eye.

Close your eyes and focus on the object while counting from 1 to 10. (The object has become a 'thought' for you.)

Ensure no other thought crosses your mind while 'seeing' the object in your mind's eye and counting from 1 to 10.

Take note of your successful attempts. 10 successful attempts are OK for a day.

Do this consistently for ten consecutive days or until you are comfortable with seeing the object in your mind's eye.

4. **Focus on the Spirit of God within you**

Repeat the relaxation exercise above.

Imagine God to be whatever you want Him to be and wherever you want Him to be. He is the Creator of the Universe and everything that is in it. For me, at times I imagine Him as the heaven (sky), or the wind, or as a spoken word.

Whatever you choose, close your eyes and see Him in your mind's eye.

Exercise 3

It is expected that at this stage you are able to control your thoughts and hold an image in your mind's eye for a prolonged period of time

This time around, you do not want to hold your thoughts.

While focusing on your chosen image of what God is within your mind's eye, you want to listen and take note of ANYTHING that drops into your mind during that period. If nothing drops into your mind, you are still OK.

With more practice, you may not have to close your eyes or be in a quiet place before you are able to connect and listen to the Spirit of God within you. You will be able to connect anywhere and anytime.

Making a request and getting a response

Make a request to God.

- Make a statement; write it down or say it aloud. Let it be very clear in your mind with no ambiguity. Focus on this for some time.

- Go about your daily activities if you need to.

- Be relaxed and be confident that you will get a response.

- Be observant and aware of what is going on around you. At times, the response to your request may be found there.

Repeat step 4 above.

(Disclaimer: while this is something I have practiced over time and works for me, the result may not be the same for everybody. Please ensure you are not acting on anything dangerous that may drop into your mind.)

Exercise 4

BE KIND TO YOURSELF. BE KIND TO OTHERS

Give YOURSELF a touch of kindness through your C.L.A.S.™

Spread a torch of kindness and make someone S.W.A.G.™

- **Give YOURSELF a TOUCH of kindness**

The acronym **C.L.A.S.** is discussed below:

C=CONVERSATIONS: **Your silent conversations**

What do you say to yourself during your silent conversations? The unspoken words that form in your mind to yourself are a direct reflection of who you believe yourself to be. Catch yourself fast as soon as you find yourself slipping into a negative conversation with yourself.

L=LAUGH: Laugh at yourself

If you find yourself in an embarrassing situation, make a joke about it and laugh out loud.

A=APPRECIATE: Think of something good about yourself and appreciate yourself

List 10 good things about yourself on a piece of paper and look at it at least twice in a day. Most of the time, the grass is always greener on the other side of the fence. We usually do not see something good about ourselves hence we feel empty and useless.

S=SMILE: Put on a smile, it costs you nothing

Put on a smile today and surround yourself with a positive aura. You are sending out positive vibrations into the universe.

- **Spread a torch of kindness**

The acronym **S.W.A.G.** is discussed below:

S=SMILE: Make someone SMILE

Make someone smile; if you can take it further, make someone laugh.

W=WORD: Say a kind WORD

Say a kind word to someone today and be sincere about it.

A=APPRECIATE: APPRECIATE someone

Has anyone done an act of kindness to you in the past? Try to remember this and appreciate the person for it. Take one person at a time and do this consistently; one person a day or one a week or one a month.

G=GOOD: The GOOD in others

Look for something good in someone today and let them know about it.

"People may not remember exactly what you did, or what you said, but they will always remember how you made them feel"

—Maya Angelou

Please visit: www.SunshineInTheMidstOfTheStorm.com/HappyLight to join the Happiness movement.

Exercise 5

COMPARTMENTALIZE YOUR RELATIONSHIPS

The aim of this exercise is to help you put in perspective and re-define your relationships so that you know who you should be interacting with most of the time

- Write down a list of 20 people you interact with; either physically, on the phone, or on social media.

- On a scale of 1 – 10, how closely do you interact with them? 1 being least close and 10 being very close.

- Looking at the characteristics of a toxic relationship in Key 5 of this book. Is there any among them you feel you are in a toxic relationship with? Put an 'X' in front of the name.

- Looking at the characteristics listed for people in Compartments 1 to 3 in Key 5, place each person you have put on scale 5 – 10 in bullet 2 above into the appropriate compartment.

Bonus: Visit www.SunshineInTheMidstOfTheStorm.com to download a free template for the above exercises.

Exercise 5

How do your compartments look like? What do you think about your relationships? Do you feel you need to make some changes in your relationships?

For more information about our programs and webinars, please go to www.SunshineInTheMidstOfTheStorm.com/Programs

CONCLUSION

Happiness is your birthright. You deserve to be happy. Even if you are going through tough times or a storm in your life, you deserve to be happy. Happiness is a CHOICE you have to make because challenging situations will pop up in your life at one point in time or another. Decide and take a stand for happiness because happiness breeds success.

Be intentional about the type of thoughts you allow in your mind. Your thoughts affect your reality. Negative thoughts reflect in negative emotions; and cause low vibrations and a negative aura around you. If you want to be happy, intentionally fill your mind with thoughts of happy events and you will attract more events that will make you happy.

Be aware that offense will come in different forms and from different people. Situations probably beyond your control may arise that will make you unhappy. Decide from now on that nothing and no one will steal your happiness. In the midst of your challenges, create happy moments for yourself and intentionally turn negative events into positive ones for yourself. By doing this, you will get out of negative situations faster.

Decide on whom you want yourself to be and allow no one and no situation turn you into something else. Life is a matter of your perspective. It is your turn to be happy. So my Friend, say to yourself, "It is my turn to be happy." "It is my turn to be happy."

Conclusion

Be calm. Move on with hope in your heart and create your world with your words and with your thoughts.

I love you.

Made in the USA
Columbia, SC
04 July 2017